WOMEN
WHO AIN'T
AFRAID
TO *Curse*
WHEN COMMUNICATING WITH GOD:

WOMEN WHO AIN'T AFRAID

TO *Curse*

WHEN COMMUNICATING WITH GOD:

A 31-Day Self-Study Guide to Spiritual Liberation

Trelani Michelle

FUNDAMENTAL

FUNDAMENTAL

Women Who Ain't Afraid to Curse When Communicating With God:
A 31-Day Self-Study Guide to Spiritual Liberation

Published by: So Fundamental Publications™

Printed in the United States of America

ISBN-10:0988625164
ISBN-13:978-0-9886251-6-7

Special discounts are available on bulk quantity purchases by book clubs, associations and special interest groups.
For details email: Info@SoFundamental.com.

For more information, log onto
www.SoFundamental.com

OTHER BOOKS BY THIS AUTHOR

What the Devil Meant for Bad

Getting Across

Getting Over

Purple Petals: Letters to Self

DEDICATION

I dedicate this book to the three-year-old me, grinning at whoever stood behind the camera telling me to say cheese. To the five-year-old me who escaped her grandparents at the airport and hid out in the car in hopes that they'd just turn around and drive us all back home. The six-year-old me who got a whipping for using a word that she didn't know the meaning of. The nine-year-old me who saved all of her lunch money to buy a diary with a key from the school's book fair. The ten-year-old me who crushed on girls way before boys entered her peripheral. The eleven-year-old me who believed her grandmother's promise that her cancer had turned into ashes. The twelve-year-old me who wondered if it was possible to be without a father's love even though she had two of them.

The thirteen-year-old me who questioned if what happened could be considered rape since she had run away from home. The fourteen-year-old me who wrote letters from youth detention centers. The fifteen-year-old me who tried her damnedest to be a good Christian. The sixteen-year-old me who got her first abortion. The seventeen-year-old me who delivered her first child. The eighteen-year-old me who experienced her first real heartbreak. The nineteen-year-old me who was so full of pride that she worked three jobs and went to school instead of asking for help. The twenty-year-old me who smoked herself from a size six to a size zero. The twenty-one-year-old me who had her second child and decided to give Christianity another shot. The twenty-two-year-old me who exchanged being a child of god for being her own woman. The twenty-three-year-old me who began her journey of self-love. The twenty-four-year-old me who got married to feel validated. The twenty-six-year-old me who got her second abortion. The twenty-seven-year-old me who finally embraced the fullness of her spirituality, sensuality and sexuality.

I dedicate this book to the woman I am now and the woman I'll become.

I love you all and not for a second am I ashamed of you. Keep living, baby.

TABLE OF CONTENTS

HOW TO USE THIS GUIDE

This guide contains 31 self-guiding studies. Each consists of a Spirit quote, warm-up prompt, introspective lesson, and suggested meditation. Prompts and meditations require several spiritual practices including visualization, journaling, breathing exercises, dancing, chanting, mirror work, and even masturbation. They are used as means of self-inquiry, intention-setting, emotional release, and chakra balancing.

You will need:

- A space where you feel comfortable doing the above-mentioned activities

- A pen and notebook

- A calendar

- A mirror

- A timer

- At least 30 minutes reserved for each study

The prompts are designed to get you in the groove for the study and to initiate self-exploration. Most of them call for writing. Though we have digital options, your unique handwriting allows for far more spiritual access and fewer distractions. The activity from the prompt leads you directly into the lesson, which is that aha, if you will. It's meant to give you the *why* behind the work. Afterwards, we flow right into either a resting or active meditation.

Begin resting meditations by sitting or lying comfortably, and relax your eyes. They may be open or closed depending on personal comfort. Engage in deep breathing to calm your thoughts and settle your awareness. During meditation, we may use a mantra, which is a repeated sound, word, or statement; a visualization, which is using your imagination; or simply focus on the flow of your breathing. If you're new to meditation, aim for 10-minute sessions. If you're more seasoned, make 20 minutes your minimum. You may use a timer, which I do, so passing time isn't a distraction.

Following this guide from front to back isn't necessary. Feel free to flip to a random page or browse the table of contents for a lesson you feel fits in that particular moment. What I want you to remember most is that this is your experience. Freak it how you see fit. :)

Ready?

GREETINGS

Telling stories has always been a passion of mine. I remember lining up my siblings and dolls to read to them my imagination's latest thriller. I also made up biographies about random passersby in the mall and remixed my favorite books. One of my favorites was *Alexander and the Terrible, Horrible, No Good, Very Bad Day*. I'd exchange Alexander for either my sister or me and use our own crappy circumstances, like having to sit at the table until we cleaned our plates or getting knockoff shoes instead of name brand.

While my imagination was abundant, my curiosity was just as grand. I wanted to know why the moon followed me, if swallowing a watermelon seed would actually put a baby in my belly, and just how far heaven was past space. I now recognize the two working in tandem—imagination and curiosity—to be necessities to storytelling. The unrelenting pursuit of knowledge and the ability to create was critical to making sense of my inner and outer worlds. Whenever I couldn't understand something, I just made it up—created stories. When my grandmother died, I reasoned that at least now her spirit would always be with me. That worked for me as a child by making the world less scary and confusing; and now,

1

as an adult, I still use the two to help me understand religion.

I'm not the first to do this. Storytelling is an ancient art form. When humans began to question how we got here and who created us, our answers came from stories. Whatever we didn't know, we made up.

The imaginary god my grandmother and Sunday school taught me as a child made absolutely no sense. He was a walking dead contradiction. I didn't understand the Holy Trinity, either, the belief that there's a son, a father, and a Holy Spirit. The son and the father were above humanity, yet given human qualities. What did that mean? I couldn't picture them. Spirit, I could. Spirit showed up and showed out every Sunday at church when one of the members would break out into a shout and race down the aisle. But God? His heaven didn't excite me, but his hell scared the shit out of me so I fumbled along anyhow. The older I got, the more I felt like I was already living in hell. Being accustomed to it, my fear of eternal burning dissipated.

By the time I was 12 I quit praying. I was tired of how unattached, repetitive, and inauthentic it felt. I craved a different perspective and was curious how others lived. I started hanging out with people who didn't go to church and watching shows that came on way after my bedtime.

I preferred this way of life to religion. Being religious was like having more parents with far more rules of what I could and couldn't do. I couldn't wait to be free, to have somewhere else to lay my head.

Unable to be or feel free, journaling was my best solution. It's where I carried my curiosities, completed my thoughts, wrote my poetry, started my fiction, and dreamed about a life that was worlds away from the run-of-the-mill, no-soul-having one that I was living.

One night, not too long ago, a monsoon of sadness washed over me. My romantic relationship was in off mode, bank account was in the negatives, job wasn't at all secure, baby was colicky, and I was missing my grandmother. I decided to journal and found myself writing a letter to God. I felt hopeless and needed to give him a piece of my mothafucking mind. (It still makes the hairs on my arms stand up to say that.) The moment was so intense that, afterward, I fell into the deepest sleep I've ever had. After a conversation like that, I couldn't go back to a fake-ass, god-fearing existence. Something had stirred inside of me. It's like my ancestors started nodding like, "Yep, she's ready."

When I broke down that night, although I had confronted the man who demanded that the g in his name be capitalized, it was Spirit who comforted me. Spirit, who had moved me as a child in church, who I felt we were all praying to and worshipping, a maternal presence, a force that shows up uniquely for every being. In my confrontation, Spirit didn't mind my anger or even my cursing because I surely didn't try to soften what I really wanted to say. I spoke what was on my heart in the exact way that it showed up for me and I felt celebrated for it. That's when my real relationship with Spirit started, and through her, my relationship with God. Until about a month ago, I had never shared that facet of my spirituality with anyone—let alone on social media—but one day I decided to post on Instagram:

I be wanting to speak on stuff sometimes, but Spirit be like, "Leave that shit alone, hear?" And I be like, "Yes, ma'am."

Posting that to the world was like rubbernecking before jumping into Double Dutch ropes. I had no clue how it'd be accepted once I hit send. I remember changing the wording around and taking out the word "shit," but decided to keep it the way Spirit had given it to me. I reminded myself that it's our uninhibited selves and authentic voice, how we speak when we're amongst our tribe that reaches the core of a person. That's what I'm in the business of doing.

So I posted it. And it was received well. So well that someone else decided to screenshot it, crop my name out, and repost it as if it were hers. She got damn near a thousand likes for it and tons of comments to go with it. Was I offended? Hell yes! But it's one of those things that doesn't make sense to give energy to, so I consciously chose to embrace the fact that my truth had resonated with so many souls. That sat much better.

Then Akilah S. Richards, my spiritual mentor/sister-friend, shared it with her circles. They loved it just as strongly. Akilah experiences Spirit in the way I do and texted me that I needed to be louder. I woke up the next morning to her invitation to a shared online document where she had created a 31-day outline based on both of our Instagram posts. She explained, "When I was in the space of your word-flow, many of my own Spirit-be-like moments came to me, too." She asked if fleshing it out with prompts, expanded lessons, and suggested meditations was something that I'd be interested in.

I was interested. And here I am. So far I've shared with you a brief background for how this guide came to be. Now I'd like to share the power of perspective, focusing on the positive; truth, honoring my God-self; and vulnerability, sharing my truth exactly as it comes to me. Perspective, truth, and vulnerability, along with curiosity and imagination, are all aspects of the month-long diving into your past and present self, in addition to other juicy topics that will help you explore and expand everything you embrace as reality. It's my prayer that you emerge more aware and unafraid of your power as a woman, healer, teacher, and creator.

Hard cheek kisses,

Trelani

Lesson 1.

I be wantin' to speak on stuff sometimes,
but Spirit be like, "Leave that shit alone, hear?"
And I be like, "Yes, Ma'am!"

> **PROMPT**
>
> Make a list of instances in which you tend to react too quickly to other people. Consider if and when you regret your verbal and physical actions, or lack thereof.

Intuition is our internal GPS. It tells us when, where, and how to act and with whom. For me, as a child, this voice sounded like my mama's, clear and booming. I knew when someone didn't have my best interest before they hurt me. If I ever felt endangered from someone, my intuition turned my stomach and reduced me to tears.

Intuition can have suppressors. For example, as children we were taught manners, requiring us to hug and kiss people with whom we didn't want to share affection, like that auntie who always smacked her lips on our cheeks. Suppressors force us to push down our natural desires and debilitate us from clearly knowing what's in our best interest. They can also impact views on traditional schooling practices, strict religion, abusive/oppressive relationships, etc.

Good news: As long as there is still breath in your body, your intuitive self is still present. She's still speaking. In fact, she never stopped. You just stopped listening. Come back home and reunite with the carefree, always-knowing little girl inside of you by listening to her and taking heed. Release those parental suppressors; don't let them inhibit your natural intuition.

MEDITATION

Find a quiet space clear of clutter. Get comfortable and begin taking long, deep breaths. Once relaxed, ask yourself what you want. Your answer is your intention. Now that you've set your intention, relax your eyes. Now listen. Your womb will tell you which thoughts are distractions and suppressors and which are wisdoms and intuition. Just listen. Afterward, go back to the list you created in your prompt and journal about ways to integrate more of this intention into that list.

Lesson 2.

Power of Knowing and Creating Change

"You do know you've got options, right?" –Spirit

PROMPT

1. Name one area of your life where you feel stuck.

2. List detailed options to get unstuck.

3. List your fears beginning with "What if."

4. List solutions to those fears.

5. Choose the option that feels best and create a scheduled to-do list for getting unstuck.

My favorite and most memorable course in undergrad, by far, was Intro to Philosophy. It was the first class that required me to do such deep introspection, to put the textbook down and actually think about what I believed and why I believed it. The values I entered with were questioned and shaken up.

The professor asked the class what it would mean to us if we learned that God did not exist. "What would you do differently, if anything at all?" she asked. A huge part of me felt relieved that I wasn't the only one thinking this way. The last bit was a tad unnerved because if there was no god, then who would I pray to when shit went haywire? In summary, she proposed that the absence of an external deity pointed the finger back to us. How does that sit with you?

Your choosing to read this book says that you've already embraced philosophy, that you were ready to be a *knower* and no longer a believer. Being stuck is an option. Walk in that truth. *Know* your power and responsibility in creating change and the life you wish to live. *Know* that you deserve it and that everything you need to obtain it, you either have already or you haven't yet taken.

MEDITATION

Place your hands over your womb and verbally express everything you want beginning with "I want." (I want to feel sexier. I want a bigger house. I want to finish my book. I want....) Keep going until you're out of things to say.

Next, place your hands over your belly button and verbally express everything you will do, beginning with "I will." (I will eat healthier. I will have more money. I will finish my book. I will....) Keep going until you're out of things to say.

Lesson 3.

Relax, Release, Revitalize

"Some days ain't meant to be worked nor planned. Some days I need to take the wheel, and for that, I need you silent and still." -Spirit

---

PROMPT

How do you know when you need a Sabbath? What mental and physical signals alert you? How do you respond? How would you like to improve your response? How can you be more proactive?

Write about it.

Reserving time to do nothing is an act of self-care, which, as feminist activist Audre Lorde puts it, "is self-preservation, and that is political warfare." That's one of my favorite quotes. It makes me picture a woman with her fist in the air, declaring that she's going to look out for herself by any means necessary. If you're fond of fucking up her vibe, she has no choice but to let you go. Her self requires it, her peace demands it, and her happiness won't have it any other way. Because she's gone without peace and happiness, she knows the value of both and will be damned if she lets anything or anyone get in the way of that.

Your number one responsibility is preserving this time for self-care. To preserve is to protect, to maintain, and to care for. As difficult as it can be, that means you have to let go sometimes. Surrender to Spirit in silence and stillness. Release all feelings of what you should or could be doing and just be. *Being* strengthens intuition, boosts creativity, teaches you more about you, and relieves anxiety—a common consequence of living on the go.

MEDITATION

Set an intention based on your responses from the prompt, then place a hand over your navel and draw a deep breath from your belly, not your chest. Your hand should rise as you inhale. Then slowly exhale. Once you've got a rhythm going, imagine that whatever you want is what you're breathing in and all the not-it shit is what you're releasing.

Belly breathing can be done while lying, sitting, or standing. (It's one of my favorites!)

Manifestation with Moon Water

"This shit right here calls for Moon Water!" -Spirit

PROMPT

When is the next full moon? Label the day on your calendar with "Moon Water" and set an alert for it.

Water is more than just two molecules of hydrogen and one molecule of oxygen. It's more than a substance we drink for hydration. It's symbolic. "Take me to the water" means something to you, as it did your mama's mama's mama, as it did to my mama's mama's mama...

We can blend our love of magic, the moon, and water into a potion that aids manifestation. It's called Moon Water. I learned about it through a simple spirituality course, which I later discuss in this book. When I first made it, I used it to start my garden and drank it as a reminder of my promises to myself. It can also be added to bath water for relaxation, used to make tea, and reserved as "holy water," if you will.

How to make Moon Water: Simply gather some natural spring water or distilled water. Bottled water is fine, too. House it in a clear container, sage it (which is a Native American tradition of clearing negative, stale energy by kindling a bundle of cedar, sweet grass, or any other dried herb), and set your intentions for it. Place it outside in an area where it can get a full view of the full moon. (A windowsill works, too.) Make it your own experience; use crystals, stones, incense, or whatever else warms your belly. When you wake up in the morning, fetch it, and enjoy!

MEDITATION

Further activate your manifestation power, putting your intentions out into the universe to later receive them as fruition. In your journal, write about things from your past that you wanted and got. It doesn't matter if you were 2 or 20, if you bought it or if it was gifted to you. The point is that your desire was fulfilled. Sometimes we need be reminded.

Lesson 5.

"Wisdom ain't always knowing; sometimes it's listening." -Spirit

---

PROMPT

Tune in to what you need or want to know right now. In what area of your life could you really go for some God-say? Write about it and then take a moment of silence to sit with it.

It was winter 2014 when I realized I wanted to quit. None of my bite-my-tongue tactics were working. I hated waking up ridiculously early, choosing my "work clothes," then sitting in traffic for about an hour only to wear a fake-ass, tight-lipped smile all day. I wanted out. My writing gig had picked up, but it wasn't enough to replace my paycheck and I had shit to lose: a mortgage, a car title, student loans, etc.

I needed an answer, but fretting over what I should do, asking others their opinion, or creating plans B and C didn't work. An answer finally revealed itself during me-time when I consciously shoved aside my worries to focus on the positives. My mind ventured back to when I was a pregnant teenager, deathly afraid of keeping my baby after my mother threatened to put me out. I spent many nights with my face buried in a pillow. It was there that my intuition assured me that I could trust myself. She didn't let me down then, and she didn't let me down on February 28th, 2014 when I turned in my two weeks' notice.

Intuition is always present, but we aren't always mentally or emotionally available to clearly perceive that inner guidance. Most times, that deep-gut, I-know-I-can-do-this feeling is muddled in doubt. That's not to say that doubt is a bad thing because it isn't. It's there to protect us, actually, right there alongside our fears. That's where knowing the difference between the voice of intuition and the voice of doubt and fear comes in handy. You won't always know, but you can always submit to silence and solitude so that you can listen. In these moments—whether you're folding clothes, journaling, walking, playing solitaire, coloring, or whatever—you'll be able to sort through the anxiety and decide. Don't just accept your circumstance. Trust yourself and choose.

MEDITATION

Our third eye is located between our brows. It is our ability to recognize kindred (and non-kindred) spirits, show compassion, and act in our truth. When our third eye is open, we're connected to the power of intuition. One way to open and balance this chakra is through a Third Eye Meditation.

Consciously release all tension in your body through slow, deep breaths. Once relaxed, imagine an indigo ball of light radiating between your brows. Inhale balance, clarity, and knowing. Exhale confusion, disconnect, and indecisiveness.

Lesson 6.

*"**Fuck them and let that self of yours shine.**"* –Spirit

PROMPT

Consider the people in your life, your environments, and habits you own that don't align with your values. How do you plan to distance yourself from these bad vibes?

Write about it.

No one had ever taught me how to express my emotions, particularly anger, and, as a result, I became very passive-aggressive, especially in my romantic relationships. With the addition of low self-esteem, the inability to express myself made me depressed, possessive, jealous, and dishonest. To cover up, I used sex as a tactic, along with inauthentic "friendly" gestures and favors. In return, I had high expectations, and whenever life didn't go right, I had something or someone to blame. I was miserable.

Being passive-aggressive is a likely result of having experienced oppression. Ironically, passive-aggression is a form of oppression. It consists of feeling restrained, limited, silenced, exploited, abused, and marginalized. Recognizing this helps us better identify it. Recognizing your own personality type can help you determine how you end up in toxic environments and ultimately how to avoid or solve them.

The opposite of passive-aggression is assertion. This is also the best way to deal with oppressive people, environments, and habits. Assertion doesn't mean you aren't afraid. It means that, in spite of the chin trembles, tears, and deep breaths, you stand up for yourself, speak your mind and your truth, respectfully and straightforwardly ask for what you want, and are willing to let someone go for the sake of your inner peace. It doesn't matter if it's a client, family member, friend, spouse, supervisor, or mirror reflection.

MEDITATION

Your throat chakra has everything to do with taking responsibility for your needs, being willing to express yourself in all circumstances. Believe it or not, your hips are directly connected to your throat. Moving those womanly hips of yours can clear your throat chakra and give you the assertive power you need to clear toxicity.

Research hip-opening yoga poses and try a few, or turn on some music and roll those hips!

Lesson 7.

Manifesto to Loving Yourself

"I recognize oppression in all forms, especially when it's disguised as love." -Spirit

---

PROMPT

This Spirit quote is from *Radical Self-Expression Manifesto: Her How-To Guide for Self-Love*. A manifesto is putting your foot down on paper. Draft your own manifesto on standing up for your needs and asserting yourself against oppression. It can be a sentence, paragraph, page, or more.

Act according to how you want to feel. Nothing else matters. The path you decide to choose should call for self-management. You are responsible for you. While others can influence how you feel, they have no control—you do. Celebrate that!

We recognize blatant bad vibes, but there are others less detectable, particularly from those we care about. They try to be caring. Love us. We willingly share our lives with them. But what do you feel when they unload their emotional baggage off their shoulders onto yours? Bad vibes.

Energy isn't created or destroyed; it's transformed and transferred. Recognizing a bad vibe is the first step. The second is choosing what to do with it and how to respond. Focusing on the negative summons more negativity. Focusing on the positive summons more positivity. Choose wisely. Start with what you're grateful for.

MEDITATION

Place your hands over your heart and verbally express everything you love about yourself and your life beginning with "I love." (I love my eyes. I love my brilliant mind. I love how far I've come. I love my big dreams. I love....") Keep going until you're out of things to say. Challenge yourself to name at least 10 things.

Lesson 8.

"Refuse to confuse desire with necessity, especially when it comes to being understood."
-Spirit

> ## PROMPT
>
> At the top of your page write "I desire to be understood, however...." Complete your thought.

One of my spiritual mentors and favorite writers, Gloria Steinem, read the words off my heart when she said that being misunderstood by people whose opinions you value is absolutely the most painful experience. When I sent my debut novel, *What the Devil Meant for Bad*, to authors whose opinions I very much valued, at least half of them told me it wasn't a good idea. They weren't saying there were holes in my plot or that my characters weren't fully developed; they were telling me to soften the edges. Because it was Christian-based, they felt that I needed to remove the profanity and sex scenes. However, to do that would have meant altering the way that Spirit gave the story to me. The mere thought of doing so made me feel like I was being

24

unfaithful to myself. I couldn't and wouldn't allow their well-meaning opinion to redirect my purpose.

Maybe you were outright rejected, ignored, or discouraged. Self-validation is key in the path of enlightenment. If you aren't careful, naysayers will have you thinking your truth is insufficient and your perspective is off. The last word is always yours. When you find yourself in that space again, repeat the prompt.

MEDITATION

Briskly rub your hands together to heat 'em up. Begin massaging your abdomen, above your navel (Solar Plexus) and below it (Sacral Chakra), to activate and enhance your personal power, self-esteem, and confidence.

Lesson 9.

"You may not always know what's wrong, but I'll make damn sure you'll know when it ain't right." -Spirit

PROMPT

Think back to a time when *it* didn't feel right. You didn't know exactly what *it* was, but you knew it wasn't right. What happened? Who was involved? How did you react? What was the result of that reaction?

Write about it.

I think I was about 16 when a friend invited me to tag along for a night out with some of her other friends. When she asked, I agreed. As time grew closer to our evening out, I got the strong urge to stay home--not because my introverted preferences took over (which they're known to do), but because it just wasn't sitting right in my gut. While getting dressed, I felt so nauseous I thought I'd vomit. When she called to say they were on the way, tears welled up in my eyes. I couldn't explain the feeling, but I just knew that I had better not go. I now

26

recognize what happened. My intuition was protecting me.

I don't always listen to my intuition. This is dangerous. I once went into an interview for a job that didn't feel right, got the job, and accepted it despite the bad vibes. Long story short, I was cornered in the back of a walk-in freezer and sexually assaulted. That's not to say that what happened was my fault, but it is to say that it could have possibly been avoided.

That feeling you just wrote about in your prompt? Mind it! Listen to it because you may not always know what's wrong, but Spirit will make damn sure you'll know when it ain't right.

"You must always be open in your spirit because, as women, our strength is the spiritual realm. You know we always feel things from our wombs." -Queen Afua, holistic practitioner and spiritual teacher

MEDITATION

Lie on your back and butterfly your legs, pressing the soles of your feet together (as comfortably as you can). Using your palms, gently press down on your womb and release. Go in rhythm with your breath as you pump life-energy into your sacral chakra.

Lesson 10.

"You say you want that life, but all I see is caution and pause. Mixed messages, Mama." - Spirit

---

PROMPT

This is another Spirit quote of Akilah's. Before you can manifest a vision, you have to be able to see it and feel it. Let's do that by first setting the tone: turn on some music to match the mood. Hear your vision, smell it, see it, touch it, and taste it. Consider who's there with you. Where are you? What else does the manifested vision consist of?

Write about it.

Determine if your vision is something that you want to do (an interest), or if it's something that you're going to do (an intention). No judgment. Just truth. A simple way to tell the difference is acknowledging whether energy is involved, or not. We already have energy moving toward intentions, but only muse occasionally about interests. However, interests can

29

become intentions the moment we put them on our to-do lists.

Intentions are what you post on the wall, make a vision board out of, visualize during meditation, etc. Once you're clear on that, you're able to give it more focus. And because you're spending less time on the not-it-shit, you'll have more time and energy for the it-shit! In fact, it'll happen. That's not to say that you won't accomplish your interests, they're just not at the forefront of your mentality right now.

If you decide that your prompt's vision is an intention but you still feel stuck, then consult with Spirit. What does your intuition say about it? If she says it's a no-go, then stop. If it aligns with your values and desires, then it's time to choose freedom over fear, which serves to protect you. At any moment, however, you can choose otherwise, in spite of its presence.

MEDITATION

Place two fingers between your eyebrows and verbally express everything you foresee beginning with "I see." (I see prosperity. I see wellness. I see global travels. I see....) Keep going until you're out of things to say.

Place your hands on the crown of your head and verbally express everything you know, beginning with "I know." (I know I'll be great. I know I'll finish my book this year. I know my marriage will heal. I know....) Keep going until you're out of things to say.

Lesson 11.

Balancing Activity with Rest in Daily Life

"Sit yo' ass down somewhere, especially when it's storming." -Spirit

> **PROMPT**
>
> Make a daily to-do list for the next three days, or look over the one you've already made. Reserve an even balance of time in your schedule for being active (exercising) and being still (meditation).

While writing your to-do list, did you feel you had to search for timeslots reserved for meditation? Can you see how much you're overextending yourself, neglecting self-care, or leaving little room for your goals?

Being busy will have you feeling like there aren't enough hours in the day. It'll end your day with migraines and backaches, and send you to bed with anxiety. When we think of everything we have to do, we leave a lot off. Busyness doesn't prioritize; it does a little bit of this and little bit of that, hoping that it adds up to completion before the deadline. It says stuff like, "I'll sleep when I die." It's exhausting, overwhelming, sickening, ineffective, and over-fucking-rated. When you're busy, your mind is too loud to hear Spirit.

You need to fall back. You need to organize and prioritize. Creative types tend to be messy—I get that and believe that—but inner-peace has a hard time settling when your surroundings are a mess. Begin simple by incorporating moments of stillness within your to-do lists. Create balance. Create productivity.

Being productive, instead of busy, helps to prioritize needs and focus on them one at a time. It clears away the busy-mess. Respect yourself with a balanced to-do list with breaks throughout the day. Challenge yourself not to think of everything of you "should be" doing instead of relaxing. Taking time-outs to tune into your feelings and work out the tension from your body will allow you to refuel, realign, and give Spirit the space to speak.

MEDITATION

Engage in a few yoga poses, or just stretch, relaxing your mind. Make the intention that you will infuse rest into your daily activities. Talk yourself through it. For example, my self-talk goes something like this: "Don't forget to breathe, Trelani...Be graceful with yourself...Take your time...Don't force it."

Lesson 12.

"...then there will be nights when you can't stop."
–Spirit

PROMPT

Many of us are most creative and productive late at night. Others prefer early morning. Some midday. Where do you stand? How do you make room for it?

Write about it.

Once upon a time, I would jump out of bed if a great idea struck me. I could hardly make it through a meditation session because I kept interrupting myself to work on my new light bulb moment. I'd sacrifice sleep when I was exhausted and time with my loved ones that I'd already reserved for us. I thought I was acting in the name of ambition, but was actually acting from a space of what-if. I feared that if I didn't get to work, I'd forget my big idea. When one would hit me, I responded in a 9-1-1 fashion. My actions revealed that inspiration didn't come around too often and that my ideas were fleeting.

Granted, there were beautiful nights when ideas did stick and my flow wouldn't quit. The more I honored those nights, the more I respected sleep and time with my loved ones.

Respect your flow. I mean that in two ways: 1. Respect it enough to know that it'll be there. You don't have to neglect yourself or abandon your values in the name of creativity. That defeats the purpose. 2. Focus on your flow. If you know the Internet is too distracting, turn it off. If other ideas come to you, jot them down somewhere, but quickly return to your initial task.

When you're flowing, your inner child is at play, making it easy to lose track of time. There's nothing wrong with that, but don't let it interrupt other reserved time. Set a timer if necessary. However, if you've set aside a large amount of time for flowing, don't forget to take breaks, stretch every now and then, and stay hydrated. If you're a snacker, keep some raw fruit and nuts on hand.

MEDITATION

Set an alarm for seven minutes, open your journal, and write. You can't stop, pause, or erase. Just write. Whatever comes to mind goes on paper. After a while of writing in this fashion (freewriting), you'll find that you've moved your mind out of the way and have let Spirit take over. If you're having trouble getting started, then write "I know" at the top of your paper, finish the sentence, and keep writing until the alarm goes off.

Lesson 13.

"You've been in your Golden Years since the day you were born." -Spirit

---

PROMPT

Set the timer for five minutes, then make a list of words that come to mind when you think of living your golden years, the period of life when you feel you have time and freedom to accomplish anything. Afterward, pick three that resonate with you the most. They could be what you wrote first, those that keep repeating themselves, or ones that just speak to you. Make a simple plan of how you can integrate those three words—or the feeling of them—into your present.

Even as a child, I understood the fault in my parents saying they couldn't wait until we (my siblings and I) moved out so they could live their life. I see the same problem in my generation delaying traveling the world until they retire. All of us, if we can be honest, hold this grand vision of a great big ol' future when we'll have all that we want to do what we want, when the fruits of our labor will have paid off.

It's important, however, to see the glory in the right now. More specifically in the back then, the right now, and the later. Don't just view the present as a transition. Feel it. Experience it. Document it. This really hit home for me when my five-old-year, Kobe, mentioned that she couldn't wait to be grown. I nudged her to love being five because this year will never come back again. Then love being six, seven, and so on.

There is no future to wait for. If you think about it, later on is technically non-existent. All we have is right now. You've been in your golden years since the day you were born. Speak and act accordingly.

MEDITATION

Grounding is the act of connecting with Mama Earth in order to harmonize our energy, get our heads out of the clouds, and back into a place of purpose where shit gets done. One of the easiest and most empowering ways to ground yourself is to plant your bare soles in nature. Go for a barefooted walk in a grassy park, take a trip to the beach, hike a trail, etc.

Lesson 14.

"Silence, when used out of fear, will deafen you inside and muffle your intuition."

-Spirit speaking to Akilah S. Richards

PROMPT

When was the last time you had to bite your tongue? When you so badly wanted to say what the fuck was your mind, but swallowed the words instead? Where were you? To whom were those digested syllables intended?

Write about it.

I pulled into a parking lot, put the car in park, and expectantly broke into tears. I had no problems in my marriage, business, health, or family, so I couldn't figure out why. I was depressed for about three weeks afterward. I scheduled an appointment with a therapist, who diagnosed me with adjustment disorder.

Many women unknowingly go through adjustment disorder. It's the feeling of despair over the course of three months or less (any longer means the problem is something else) after you've power-driven through a number of life changes without taking time to process and release.

Up until that point, I hadn't done any processing or releasing of tragedy in my life; I hadn't even really talked about it. So while I thought that all was well, in actuality, all was suppressed. I had bitten my tongue too many times. I had needed to renegotiate terms with my top-paying client, but feared the what-ifs. I was long overdue for a woman-to-woman with my mother, but feared disturbing the peace. I had needed to reintroduce myself, if you will, to my husband, but feared he wouldn't understand.

My breakdown wasn't random at all. I'd been hurting all along. Though aware of Audre Lorde's warning that silence doesn't protect, and of Zora Neale Hurston's that if you're silent about your pain, they'll kill you and say you enjoyed it, I didn't think they applied to me. Now I know better. Biting my tongue was only fucking me up inside. Following my needs with "but" was muffling my intuition, as it could do with yours.

MEDITATION

Take a shower and verbally express all of your suppressed truths. The draining water is fear and confusion; the running water is courage and clarity. Make sure to speak out loud.

Lesson 15.

Uncovering Your Universal Magic

"Good thing I don't employ repossession tactics, because I gave you so much magic you refuse to use, and I might just..."

-Spirit speaking to Akilah S. Richards

PROMPT

In what area of your life are you playing small or settling? Write about it then engage in some #MirrorWork. It's time to reintroduce you to yourself. Remind yourself who you are and the power you have.

You may not be Superwoman, but you definitely have super powers. When you see growth as your default and freedom as your divine right, you can achieve freedom to go and do and buy and try and fly as you please. You can shift obstacles into opportunities! Problems into solutions!

I'm a huge optimist and often joke that my hope will be the death of me. My life experiences have taught me that if I align my actions with desires—be it a man, a mentor, a trip, a house—it's mine. The same access I have, you

43

have too. We're all connected to the same source energy, but just have to keep ourselves grounded to tap into it. We have to understand our relationship with this world, and surround ourselves with those who inspire us to love harder, think bigger, and speak louder.

Don't just believe you can. *Know* you can. Know your value and your worth. Make your thoughts work for you. Your thoughts are your truth. Your truth is your vibe. And your vibe is what attracts everything and everyone you need to get from where you are to where you want to be. That's your magic.

MEDITATION

Mindfulness will keep you grounded in your power. Cultivate your awareness by integrating it in your everyday tasks. Instead of being caught up in busy thoughts or rushing from the present, aim to be fully engaged while eating, moisturizing, washing dishes, bathing, etc. Choose a task and try it now.

$\mathcal{L}esson\ 16.$

"Don't try to pin that shit on me. I don't send tests for my people, I send resources."

–Spirit speaking to Akilah S. Richards

PROMPT

At the top of your paper write "God is...." Now set your timer for seven minutes and free write.

One thing that I wish would die, be buried and never resurrect, is the idea that God sends trials and tribulations our way to test our spirit. That god is not for you, and it's time to release it. As Akilah would say, "That's some slave shit!" No one is sending any tests, and there is no devil.

Sometimes the enemy is you, and until you stop to assess how you contributed to the situation, it'll continue to happen. Those same "tests" will keep circling back around. This may be hard to swallow, but it's true. You have to own it by taking responsibility for your part in it. Granted, some things are happenchance, but, even then,

45

your reaction to them makes the difference. You always have a choice.

On the other side of the coin, you also deserve the glory for the achievements. Pinning your success on anyone or anything outside of yourself takes your power away. You did that! You earned that! With the help of your ancestors—yes; with the help of Spirit—yes; with the help of the resources that Spirit sent your way—yes. Listening and reacting effectively—this was all you. Yes.

MEDITATION

Repeat the following meditation until each word resonates in your being:

I am power, housing creation and intuition. Therefore, I am all-knowing. I heal myself with words of truth. I am whole, in search of higher. I am she who came and she who comes. Divinely aligned, I am exactly who I wanted to be. I am power.

Lesson 17.

"Start with an apology." –Spirit

PROMPT

At the top of your page write your name followed by I'm sorry. For example: "Trelani, I'm sorry." Now complete your apology.

Growing up, my dad constantly reminded me not to say that I was "sorry" because that was like saying that I was pathetic, but to say that I apologize instead. As I've grown older, however, I've realized how much feeling is in saying sorry. It reaches a part of the subject that "I apologize" misses every time. We owe ourselves so many sorrys—whether it's for what we physically did, allowed, said, or thought.

As Tiny Buddha blogger, Lori Deschene said best, "We can't hate ourselves into another version of ourselves we'll love." You're resting on Spirit's lap, your head against her breast, her hand pulling you closer, and she's rocking you. She doesn't ask what's wrong or who hurt you because she knows. She only asks that you

47

apologize, to say you're sorry, so that you can begin filling that space with love.

MEDITATION

Sit on your hands and verbally express everything you are, beginning with "I am." (I am beautiful. I am creative. I am loving. I am....) Keep going until you're out of things to say.

Lesson 18.

Cursing, Passion, and Truth

*"Give it to them exactly the way I gave it to you.
Just like so."* –Spirit

PROMPT

Select your favorite curse word, or the one that first comes to mind, and use it in a creative title. Beneath this title, write a poem, short story, or some other type of creative writing.

What's the difference between your lover saying, "I love you so much" verses, "I love you so fucking much"? Passion! The *umpf* behind the words lights something up in you. That's how conversations with Spirit ought be—passionate and authentic. Avoid what should be said and how it should be said, and spit it the way it comes to you. Keep it real.

A few years ago, I volunteered to lead creative writing workshops in a local middle school. The first day of class the students made it verbally clear that they didn't want to be there. For about two weeks, I had trouble getting them to write anything. By week three, I took a risk and had them write a letter to the person they were most upset with, as if they were actually speaking to the person and were guaranteed not to be punished for anything they said. The most difficult part of that assignment was helping them choose one person. Otherwise, they flowed as if all they needed was permission to be themselves.

Journaling is where we complete our own thoughts and make sense of what we're thinking. We love it because it's for our eyes only; no one can be offended. There's no harm in journaling, only truth, our personal truth. Your personal truth is your lighted path to liberation. Journaling is the starting point—as I surely prefer writing out my thoughts before verbally sharing them with someone else. However, once you begin speaking it and sharing it, then you begin the real healing process, which leads to you building your platform, attracting your tribe, and living your purpose.

Independence begins with "in" (with "in" = within). Before we can expect the world to accept us for who we are, to free us to radically express ourselves, we have to do so first. We have to shed ourselves of the disclaimers and euphemisms. No more sugarcoating. As poet, Nayyirah Waheed scribed, "When you are struggling in your writing, it usually means you are hearing one thing, but writing another."

MEDITATION

Sit or lie comfortably and focus your attention onto your heart. Imagine that you're breathing from your heart and start affirming all that you trust beginning with "I trust." (I trust who I am. I trust my intuition. I trust....) Some affirmations may call for repetitions. That's cool. Keep going until you're out of things to say.

Lesson 19.

Unearthing Self-Perception

"You are not messy. You are magic." –Spirit

PROMPT

What's one area of your life that you consider yourself to be a mess? Flip it and find the magic in it. Write about it.

I was in one of my gotta-get-it-done cycles when one of my sister-friends, Katrina "Belu Sage" Harrell, sent myself a few others one of those beloved "because it was on my heart to say it" emails. The last line of it read, "You are not messy. You are magic." I needed to hear that in that moment because though my energy was high, my vibrations were extremely low. My mind was stuck on everything that wasn't going right. I was violating one of my own entrepreneurial commandments which stated that I wouldn't downplay my talent based off of a few projects that didn't go as planned.

But it wasn't just my work. It seemed to be everything around me, which, in retrospect, makes sense because when you focus on the mess, that's all that'll show up for you. It's all about perspective and how you perceive

52

yourself is important. I strongly believe in the power of affirmations, of building yourself up by deciding for yourself who you are. Unless you get to the root of the negative thoughts about yourself, then affirming will only go so far.

After being diagnosed with adjustment disorder, one of my processes of releasing included going all the way back, as far as I can remember, and writing down what I remember. As we get older, these highlighted moments lessen, but some never go away. And regardless how trivial they may seem, if you still remember it, then it's for a reason. Maybe it was what someone said to you, how they looked at you, or what they did to you. Maybe a particular happening didn't have the outcome that you expected and it hurt you more than you thought it did.

Going backwards to unearth why you think of yourself the way you do—even if the thought comes and goes—is fundamental in your ability to genuinely see yourself as magic, as beautiful, as gifted, and as a perfectly perfect creation who is fully deserving of your desires and equally capable of acquiring them.

MEDITATION

The prompt called for you to find the magic in what you perceive to be your mess. What color or colors come to mind when you think of yourself being magical? Are you flying, floating, swimming, running, levitating, etc.? Take a moment to bask and be.

Lesson 20.

Appreciating Mama Resources;
Appreciating Mama

"Your mama is entitled to both magic and mistakes. Give her some space to be someone besides your mama."

–Spirit speaking to Akilah S. Richards

PROMPT

Write your mother a letter starting the first line with "I free you to...." Afterward, you can choose to give it to her, bury it, burn it, give it to the ocean, or whatever sits best with your spirit. If you're led to, write another for your grandmother or any other maternal figure.

According to traditional West African belief systems, we choose our life purpose before we are even born. Knowing what that divine purpose requires, we preemptively equipped ourselves with the necessary resources to make it happen, two of which are our parents. Yet again, this points the finger back at us, to you. *You* choose your mother. You choose how to accept her, appreciate her, and love her. You choose how to value her as a resource, teaching her what you need in order to become your higher self.

Problem is, we forget that before she was our mother, she was _____ (insert her name here). Like you, she also had and has challenges and choices. And like you, she didn't and doesn't always choose what's ideal for herself or those around her. We have to remember that we are all on our own life paths and that we are all entitled to both magic and mistakes. Give her some space to be someone besides your mama.

MEDITATION

Most breathing techniques ask you to breathe in and out through your nose, but for this one, breathe in through your nose and out through your mouth. When you inhale—and take your time with it—consider what you forgive your mother for. When you exhale, visualize your breath carrying that forgiveness out of your heart and into hers.

Lesson 21.

"The words that come to you ain't just for you!"
-Spirit

PROMPT

The soul of your message is your why, which is your purpose and motivation for doing what you do. What's your why? Write about it in the form of a haiku.

You have successfully survived everything that you've gone through. All of it. Everything. And someone out there is waiting to heal through you, and she needs to hear/read/see it from you because your voice speaks her language. Stop sitting on your wisdom. It's time to turn up the volume. Louder!

In addition to clarifying your why, consider to whom your message is for and how you'd like to deliver it. If you've been speaking or writing for a while now, then consider how your audience or platform might expand. Let's see where it takes you. No plan is too big or small, whether it's increasing your following on Facebook, starting a YouTube channel, writing a book, becoming a TEDx speaker, or having a show on OWN. Even if you aren't a professional writer or speaker, you can still get your message out. For example, one of my goals have always been to do something for those behind bars, as well as elders in nursing homes.

When you arrive at a truth that makes your life a little easier, don't just sit on it. Share it. Plan a girl's night and suggest it to them. If you're still feeling it, go larger. You've always wanted to do it. You just have to remember what it is and do it. This ain't just a thinking exercise; write it down. As the #Baduizm goes, "Write it down on real paper with a real pencil, and watch shit get real."

MEDITATION

One of my favorite meditations is dancing solo. If you have a full-length mirror, that's even better. If not, no worries. We're celebrating your words manifesting as the love, life, light, and liberation that they are purposed to be with the ever so spiritual, sensual, and chakra-balancing act of dancing. If you haven't danced in a while, it may feel awkward in the beginning, but stick with it; you'll warm up.

Prep the room, find the right music, and maybe stretch first or consider going bare. It's not about how you look. It's about how you *feel*. Move in a way that physically feels good to you. Relaxing the hips, winding the kinks out of the lower back, and flexing the shoulders further unleash your wildish nature and give creativity and courage more space to roam.

Lesson 22.

Tuning In: Sexual Self-Satisfaction

"Your clitoris is your soul's harp.
Go ahead, Love. Tune in."

-Spirit speaking to Akilah S. Richards

PROMPT

Grab a mirror and spend some sacred one-on-one time with your poon (as my grandma called it) or china (as my daughter calls it). Open her lips and look inside. Gently lift the hood to see more of your soul's harp. If you're nudged to, oil your hands and massage her. Take a deep breath and exercise your divine right to self-pleasure. You deserve it. Plus, she's yours.

Sexual energy is creative energy, as both are housed in the sacral chakra. When this channel is imbalanced, you might find yourself people pleasing without minding your own feelings, feeling emotionally detached from yourself and those around you, having zero sex drive, suffering from a creative block, or letting yourself go (whatever that means for you).

Oh, but when it's popping?! You're genuinely happy, self-validated, aware of what you want out of life, okay with saying no to others, tuned in to your creativity, able to fully enjoy sex, and feel overall balanced. Engaging in sensual activities is the best way to keep your sacral chakra open and happy. Sensual activities includes: fetching sunlight and fresh air, going panty-less, mindfully eating raw fruits and veggies, listening to live music, drinking hot tea, getting massages, involving yourself in stimulating conversations, and shameless, unrushed solo sex sessions.

Fall in love with your vagina...again. Your woman parts ain't just for making babies and pleasing others. It's for you. From your ass to your perineum, outer lips, inner lips, opening, cervix, g-spot, and especially your clitoris and each and every one of her 8,000-and-counting nerve endings. That's all you, for your pleasure and power. Go ahead, Love. Tune in.

MEDITATION

Yoni breathing brings awareness to the pelvic area, deepens your personal relationship, and enhances your sexual/creative energy. *Really* step into your pussy power by adding an affirmation. Slowly inhale while contracting your vaginal muscles, hold it for 3-5 seconds (longer if you can), while visualizing your affirmation, then slowly release. Note: Make sure your throat, jaw and mouth are relaxed as they are directly connected to the hips and vagina.

Lesson 23.

"Who you are requires many mothers, including previous and future versions of yourself." -Spirit

---

PROMPT

What did you need from your mother that you didn't get? How did you (or are you) giving that to yourself?

Write about it.

In addition to having a mother and stepmother growing up, I also attracted other mamas, including mothers-in-law, grandmothers-in-law, nursing home patients, co-workers, and more. My purpose was so big and my passions were so loud that (now knowing) I couldn't dare expect one woman to supply all that I needed for my journey.

Thankfully, whatever stage of my life I happened to be in, a fairy godmother would show up to remind me that I was too smart and pretty to be in the streets, always have at least $20 on me, add castor oil to my shampoo, rest often and not feel guilty for it, treat my pussy better than I'd expect my man to treat it, add all my stock to my gumbo at once so the roux doesn't separate, and other goodies along those lines.

I also mothered myself and still do. Not long ago, for instance, my inner maternal voice stopped me mid-bath to slow down. She pointed out how rough I was being with my body and how I was unnecessarily rushing the process. Before going to sleep, she reminded me why it's important not to go to bed with a busy mind. In another instance, my dad said that he was coming down to visit us. Not judging him for it, but knowing how he is, my excitement begged me to put my foot down. She'd been let down before and wanted to protect my children and me from the potential disappointment. I listened to her as I listened to my motherly self, too. With all of my knowing, however, I still rely on Spirit's resources, including my many mamas, to guide me along the way.

MEDITATION

Remember that prayer is how we talk to God. Meditation is our way of listening. In the way that you pray (verbally, writing, sketching, etc.), ask Spirit what you need for the next step in your journey. Then sit and listen.

Lesson 24.

Interests vs. Intentions: Excuses vs. Choices

"Your creativity and your intuition are no longer equipped to process your deferment requests and forbearance applications."

-Spirit speaking to Akilah S. Richards

PROMPT

In what area of your life do you make the most excuses? What's the truth of the matter? How can you either step into your truth or remove yourself from the situation?

Write about it.

One of the best things I could have possibly done for my clients (and myself) was to help them determine if finishing their books was an interest or an intention. This goes for you and your ambitions, too. If you're interested, you may very well still do it—if it's convenient. If it's your intention, then you're committed and will make room for it—you'll do it what it takes to make it happen.

I first put off writing my book because I'd just had a baby and decided to wait until he got a little older. By the time he got a little older, I was in college and working full-time. I realized then that there would always be a reason not to write my book. That's not to say that our excuses aren't valid, but it is to say that if we don't find a way to work around our excuses, then we'll never transcend.

One thing about an excuse is that we usually test it out on ourselves before we try to sell it to others. We mention the excuse in passing and wait to see if we receive validation from others, pity, sympathy or empathy. We shouldn't do this. We should do the opposite of an excuse: make a choice. This means the reason you didn't get something done was because you chose not to do it. It's saying that, in spite of a long-ass to-do list and everything going on around you (and maybe even inside of you), you're holding yourself accountable. That's a big-girl-panty-wearing move right there.

You made a commitment then something came up. Life happened. What you gon' do?

MEDITATION

Go for a walk outdoors. While out, say, "I owe it to myself to _____, in spite of _____," filling the blanks with what you feel appropriate. Keep going until you're either out of things to say or you've completed your walk. Close it with a prayer.

Lesson 25.

*"Where two or three women are gathered,
I'm right there with them."* -Spirit

PROMPT

Schedule a gathering with your girls to flesh out ya'alls' intentions and desires. While you're at it, go ahead and celebrate the manifestation of everyone's intentions and desires with a ceremony. Scattered across the globe? Video chat.

Can you relate to meeting with a girlfriend or two and going way over the time that you intended to spend? I can't count how many nights my girls and I have been politely kicked out of a restaurant or coffee shop because they were closing. Our circles of sisterhood are our sacred spaces to vent, confess, brag, and be. We need one another and are so meant for one another that when we spend enough time together, our menstrual cycles sync. Is that deep, or what?

As juicy and delicious as our relationships may be with our significant others, we still require that goddess communion. If you've been hesitating to connect with your goddess tribe because you've been hurt by a woman in the past, to which I can surely relate, then I challenge you to let it go. Don't allow your past to obstruct your present, and never neglect your truth in any relationship. Vulnerability, transparency, trust, and truth are key.

As important as it is to make time to cultivate our relationships with our current sister-friends, we should also seek opportunities to stretch our circles. Network. Go back to the playground and open yourself to meeting new friends. Create more sacred spaces for women to explore and express themselves.

"She craves men but women are her most abiding lovers. Her friends are her soul mates, all the love without the consumption of sex and romance, a different kind of intimacy. Women make love by admiring each other, studying and envying each other and mixing it all up in a pot of devotion." -G.G. Renee Hill

MEDITATION

We call, text, and video chat, but when was the last time you wrote a letter? Grab a pen and paper and get emotional with it.

Lesson 26.

*"The more you tap into your You-ness,
the more of Me you'll find."* –Spirit

PROMPT

Write down 21 things that you love about your Self (inner *you*, not your body). Then write down another 21 things that you love about your physical body.

---

rediscovered me. I went back in my mind to a time I got a whipping for talking too much in school and talking back at home. Back to when I was too afraid to stand up for myself. When I hated my hair for being too nappy, my nose for being too big, and my ass for being too small. When my aunt caught me humping and called me nasty. When I felt like God damned me with a less-than status. Went back to when my mama read my diary and cried over my words.

After my travel through time, I said fuck the world, locked the door, and worked on me. I screamed and laughed and cried like a madwoman. I found my voice again. Experimented with my hair and played in my panties.

Apologized to myself and figured out how I prefer to be talked to. Gave society their God back (and I'm working on giving them their GMOs back). Realized how sexy healthy and happy looks on me. Discovered that the more I tap into my Me-ness, the closer I connect with God (as understood by me). In that space, everything I consciously and subconsciously request was answered with a bold, all-caps, italicized, lime green, exclamatory *YES*!

MEDITATION

Take a moment to bask in your glory. From your toes up to your calves, knees, hips, torso, breasts, arms, hands, collarbones, nose, eyes, and scalp. The energy you radiate and the love you vibrate: swim in that light. Settle into your magnificence.

Lesson 27.

Achieving Independent Ambitions...Independently

"I never meant for your partners to be your sources; resources, Baby."

- Spirit speaking to Akilah S. Richards

PROMPT

Identify your values by asking and answering, "What's important to me in my _____?" (Fill in the blank with what you deem appropriate: career, love life, social life, health, etc.) Doing so helps you be a leader and active participant in all areas of your life.

My co-worker and I—both aspiring authors—looked forward to the Black Writer's Conference and Retreat back in 2012, but when she cancelled, I reluctantly did too, using the excuse that it was too far out of my budget to go alone. But something kept tugging my insides, refusing to let up. I wanted to go. I had to go.

Though the deadline had passed, I emailed the director and asked her if I could still attend if I made my own lodging accommodations. She agreed. I sent her my writing samples—which was the first time someone had read my creative writing—then spent my car note and cable funds to make my first solo trip. I met my mentor and a slew of other valuable connections there and two months later, I published my debut novel.

When my co-worker couldn't come through, thank God I didn't stop the show. The same went for a project that I wanted to partner up for. Two deadlines passed before I decided that it was my idea and therefore my responsibility to manifest.

Be careful not to put too much stake in partnerships—including those with our spouses—instead of being what you want and knowing the resources will come, be it inner wisdom; a paid professional; or the right book, web series, conference, or conversation at the right time. The needed resource will come when you're ready for it. You just make sure you're open.

"A woman who walks in her purpose doesn't have to chase people or opportunities. Her light causes people and opportunities to pursue her." -Unknown

MEDITATION

"Om" is the sound of the universe. That one little syllable is the vibration of all living things. Repeating it reconnects us to this source of abundance. Take 10-20 minutes to be still, while repeating this sacred mantra.

Lesson 28.

Uncertainty, Selectivity, Love, and Self-Love

"Stepped on many toes to get back to myself."
-Spirit

PROMPT

At the top of your paper write, "The thought of it scares and excites me at the same time." What is "it" for you? Why does it scare and excite you? Complete your thought.

Life experiences had me angry, bitter, vengeful, and distrustful. I was most interested in success. It would improve my station in life, yes, but it would also allow me to look back at everyone in my past with my tongue out. This was certainly not the most productive or healthy way to think.

I remember a guy flipping out on me after he had done every single thing I requested of him to prove his affection, and yet I still didn't feel it. He asked what the fuck I wanted from him and I shrugged. "I don't know." It was a life-changing moment. I didn't know what I wanted from him, from myself, or from life. I had no clue. I was too far gone, but from what, I didn't know.

It took solitude and, in my case, poverty, to understand what I wanted. Between my fat attitude and flat wallet, I couldn't afford distractions. I would get off work and come home to an empty, silent house that almost drove me insane until I started writing again. On paper, I was God. I knew what my characters wanted, even when they didn't, and I also knew how they were holding themselves back. I later learned that fiction was (and is) my way of getting it all out without judgment. I could go back and retell the whole story in order to properly arrive at the resolution. I could learn the importance of life's plot twists.

Writing taught me how to forgive and how to rebuild my capacity to love and be loved, starting with me. The journey back to me offended a lot of people, like that past lover, but I didn't accept their anger as my concern. After all, I still had some healing to do.

Once you're on that path to finding what you love about other and yourself, which you are (yes, *you*), then you know the value of discernment. The ability to judge who and what is and is not in your best interest, and the willingness to act accordingly, is self-love. In all you do, prioritize discernment, which, oddly, teaches how to prioritize.

MEDITATION

The prompt called for you to write out one of your scary-exciting desires. Now meditate on it. Close your eyes and see it. Feel it. Bring it from the space of maybe to the place of yes.

Lesson 29.

Speaking Up For Your Beliefs

"No, baby. Get back in your feelings." -Spirit

PROMPT

What do you believe that others may not necessarily agree with? Using your journal, explore this idea with the Five Whys:

1) Why do you believe it to be true?

2) Once you respond, question this again, ask yourself why.

3) Why that?

4) And why that?

5) One more... Why? By the time you reach your fifth why, you will have arrived at your core belief.

A friend once asked me if I felt guilty for keeping the kids in the house all day. I told her that once upon a time I would have, but that, fortunately, I was—and am—at the point where I could tell my children the truth: Mama don't feel like being fun right now. I'd rather

78

just stay home or spend time alone in my room. Her response: "Sooo glad you can relate."

Say what you want to say, not what you think you should say. Ignore society telling you to get out of your feelings. That's bullshit. To tell you to shut your feelings down is to tell you to shut up. Speak your truth, even at the risk at of being misunderstood or rejected. Believe it or not, someone out there is dying to hear your point of view. Think about it: I'm sure that you can relate to the relief of knowing that you aren't alone in your thoughts, beliefs, and desires. It's a very warming and liberating feeling. You don't have to wait until it arrives. You can pop it off. Your truth is your vibe, and your vibe attracts your tribe. Feelings of shame or guilt will sure enough kill it. Don't let it.

MEDITATION

Place your hands over your throat and verbally express everything you speak, beginning with "I speak." (I speak truth. I speak up for myself. I speak against oppression. I speak....) Keep going until you're out of things to say. Challenge yourself name at least 10 things.

Lesson 30.

Anger's Place: Inflaming Change

"Some shit is gonna call for fire, plain and simple."
-Spirit

PROMPT

Write about an experience that called for immediate action or insurgency that you followed through on, one that you're proud of. Include who, what, when, where, how, and why from the experience. Your writing should be so deep into the memory that you feel it in your body.

Anger, regardless of its bad rep, is a necessary emotion. Otherwise, we wouldn't have it, right? It's designed to show us something about ourselves and incite change. Anger is what freed our ancestors from being property. Anger is what moves the political arena when polls, protests, and praying aren't cutting it. The same goes with our personal lives.

"Some shit is gonna call for fire, plain and simple." That's another one of Akilah's bomb-ass quotes. Some actions demand a reaction. It may be on your job, in your home, or out in public, but you can't afford to bite your tongue on this one or just get on the phone and vent about it. Our mothers and foremothers warned us to choose our battles. Spirit will tell you which one calls for fire. You'll know because you'll feel it. That feeling is Spirit; it's you. You are God. You are the omnipotent, omniscient deity that you've been waiting for.

Anger doesn't always call for violence. It may be speaking out against or leaving. If you're being disrespected in your workplace and decide to step over fear and speak up for yourself, (and walk the fuck out, if necessary) then you have appropriately acted on anger. The same goes for any relationship that you're in, as well as activism within your physical and online communities, as well.

"Look, I choose peace, but say...Don't walk up on me wrong. This tea and incense can turn into a Colt 45 and Newports if need be..." -Erykah Badu

MEDITATION

Think back to a time when you felt powerless. Minus self-criticism, re-experience it play-by-play. (Note: You're an observer, not a victim.) Now, using your imaginative power, recreate the story and *symbolically* take your power back. Maybe you imagine your power as a crystal, a light, your heart, etc. Place your hands on your navel and imagine the power being restored. Seal it with an "I will" affirmation (I will trust myself. I will stand up for me. I will speak against oppression in all forms. I will...).

Lesson 31.

CONCLUSION

You Deserve to Take Up Space and Wear a Crown

"Magic, me-time, mothering, moonlight, reasons to moan, and money; that about completes my list of demands."

-Spirit speaking to Akilah S. Richards

PROMPT

Start a timer for ten minutes and simply list everything you demand—now and later.

Nigerian novelist and feminist Chimamanda Ngozi Adichie blew my entire fucking mind when she reminded women that, "You deserve to take up space." You deserve a place in this world. From Father Sky to Mama Earth and everything beautiful in between, you are worthy of it. However, first you have to want it.

Get bossy with it. Desire it so hard that you demand it. That's your right, you know? Women don't have magic. We *are* magic, and our wombs are our creative center, our powerhouse, and the seat of our intuition. If you want it, you can design it, you can create it, you can live it, and you know it. As James Baldwin told us, and Oprah reminded us, "Your crown has been bought and paid for. Put it on your head and wear it."

MEDITATION

Let's put them all together, moving energy and power from your root to your crown. With all of these, keep going until you're out of things to say.

1. Sit on your hands and verbally express everything you are beginning with "I am."

2. Place your hands on your womb and verbally express everything you want beginning with "I want."

3. Place your hands over your navel and verbally express everything you will do/have beginning with "I will."

4. Place your hands over your heart and verbally express everything you love beginning with "I love."

5. Place your hands over your throat and verbally express everything you speak beginning with "I speak."

6. Place your two fingers between your eyebrows and verbally express everything you foresee and see in the present, beginning with "I see."

7. Place your hands on the crown of your head and verbally express everything you know beginning with "I know."

MERCI

I've grown so much in the process of writing this book and pray that it resonated with you just as vividly. You can use it over and over again. As you know, we move in cycles. Growing, yeah, but we also return to the same lessons. That's what I wanted this book to be—one that you could return to and even share.

Creating sacred spaces to ask, answer, relate, heal, and grow is our responsibility. It's something that I'm extremely passionate about. I knew that it would take a special kind of woman to connect with the title *Women Who Ain't Afraid to Curse When Communicating with God*, and you did. You are my tribe!

Back in Lesson 4, I promised that I'd share more info about the Finding Time for Self-Care through Simple Spiritual Rituals e-course. As the name suggests, it's totally web-based and helps you define spirituality on your own terms, set spiritual goals, create an incantation, make moon water, take your spiritual self-care to a whole 'nother level with an intense 20-day challenge, and so much more. There are over 40 lectures and you go at your own pace, having access to the other students in the course (yep, the tribe just expanded yet again). If that raises your eyebrows even just a little bit, use my affiliate link here to learn more: **http://bit.ly/myspirituality**

I used the hashtag #SpiritBeLike on social media while developing the book, as I still do now, and I now invite you to use it for your own quotes from Spirit. This way, we can easily connect with one another. *"Me and you, us never part. Makidada. Me and you, us have one heart. Makidada. Ain't no ocean, ain't no sea. Makidada. Keep my sister away from me."*

Sending you beaucoup love and light on your journey.

Warm regards,

Trelani

ABOUT THE AUTHOR

Trelani Duncan was the girl beneath the covers with a flashlight and a journal. The teenager who documented her life experiences as poetry. The college student who experimented with erotic short stories.

A true Piscean and INFP personality type, she combined her love for storytelling with that of helping others. A spiritual writing coach, she teaches women how to explore and express their unique perspective and experiences through soulful storytelling.

Learn more at SoFundamental.com, and be sure to follow her ventures on Instagram @Trelani_Michelle.

P.S. Don't forget to review this book on Amazon.com.

You're much appreciated!

Made in the USA
Middletown, DE
12 June 2016